HAL•LEONARD

JAZZ PLAY-ALONG®

Book and CD for Vocal Performance

volume
128

VOCAL
Standards
LOW VOICE

ISBN 978-1-4234-9182-8

HAL•LEONARD®
CORPORATION
7777 W. BLUEMOUND RD. P.O. BOX 13819 MILWAUKEE, WI 53213

Visit Hal Leonard Online at
www.halleonard.com

All of Me

WORDS AND MUSIC BY SEYMOUR SIMONS
AND GERALD MARKS

CALL ME IRRESPONSIBLE

FROM THE PARAMOUNT PICTURE PAPA'S DELICATE CONDITION

WORDS BY SAMMY CAHN
MUSIC BY JAMES VAN HEUSEN

AUTUMN LEAVES

ENGLISH LYRIC BY JOHNNY MERCER
FRENCH LYRIC BY JACQUES PREVERT
MUSIC BY JOSEPH KOSMA

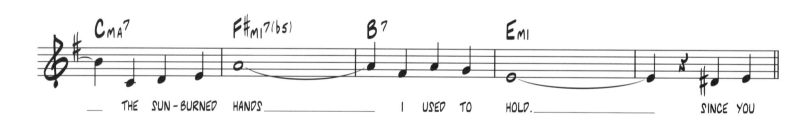

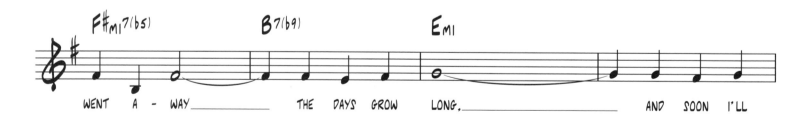

COME SUNDAY

FROM BLACK, BROWN & BEIGE

BY DUKE ELLINGTON

DESAFINADO
(OFF KEY)

ENGLISH LYRIC BY GENE LEES
ORIGINAL TEXT BY NEWTON MENDONCA
MUSIC BY ANTONIO CARLOS JOBIM

DREAMSVILLE

LYRICS BY JAY LIVINGSTON AND RAY EVANS
MUSIC BY HENRY MANCINI

GEE BABY, AIN'T I GOOD TO YOU

CD **7**

WORDS BY DON REDMAN AND ANDY RAZAF
MUSIC BY DON REDMAN

GYPSY IN MY SOUL

WORDS BY MOE JAFFE AND CLAY BOLAND
MUSIC BY CLAY BOLAND

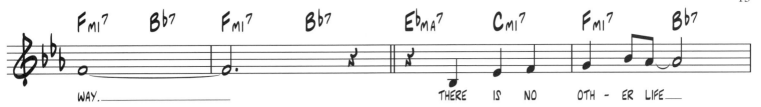

WAY._____ THERE IS NO OTH - ER LIFE____

OF WHICH I'M FOND - ER.____ IT'S JUST THE GYP - SY IN____ MY

SOUL._____ NO____ CARES!_____ NO____ STRINGS!__

_____ MY____ HEART_____ HAS__ WINGS.__

_____ IF I AM FAN - CY FREE,____

AND LOVE TO WAN - DER,____ IT'S JUST THE GYP - SY IN____ MY

SOUL._____ SOUL._____

I COULD WRITE A BOOK

FROM PAL JOEY

WORDS BY LORENZ HART
MUSIC BY RICHARD RODGERS

MY ROMANCE
FROM JUMBO

WORDS BY LORENZ HART
MUSIC BY RICHARD RODGERS

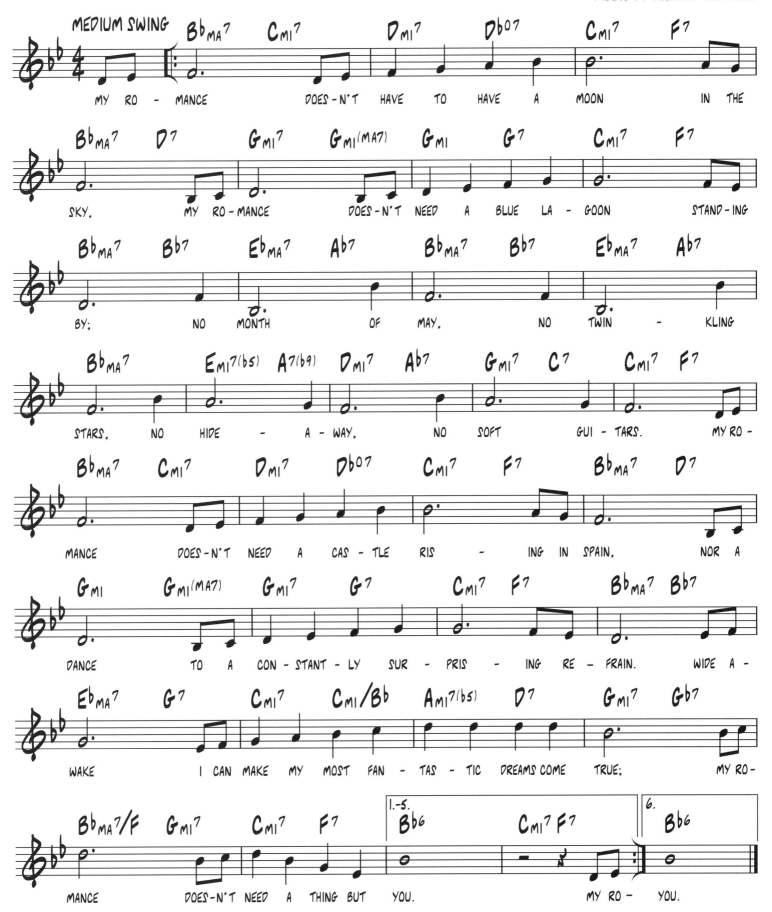

LITTLE BOAT

ORIGINAL LYRIC BY RONALDO BOSCOLI
ENGLISH LYRIC BY BUDDY KAYE
MUSIC BY ROBERTO MENESCAL

MY LIT - TLE BOAT IS LIKE A NOTE BOUNC - ING MER - RI - LY A - LONG, HEAR IT

SPLASH - ING UP A SONG. THE SAILS ARE WHITE, THE SKY IS BRIGHT, HEAD - ING

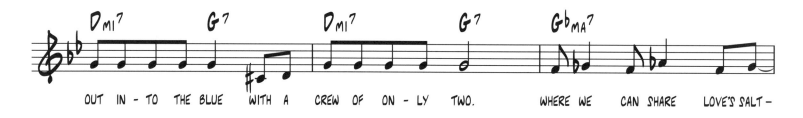

OUT IN - TO THE BLUE WITH A CREW OF ON - LY TWO. WHERE WE CAN SHARE LOVE'S SALT -

- Y AIR ON A LIT - TLE PAR - A - DISE THAT'S A - FLOAT. NOT A

CARE HAVE WE IN MY LIT - TLE

BOAT. THE WIND IS STILL, WE FEEL THE THRILL OF A

VOY - AGE HEAV - EN BOUND, THOUGH WE ON - LY DRIFT A - ROUND.

WARMED BY THE SUN, TWO HEARTS___ AS ONE BEAT - ING

WITH EN - CHANT - ED BLISS, MELT - ING IN EACH OTH - ER'S KISS.

WHEN DAY - LIGHT ENDS AND SLY - LY SENDS LIT - TLE STARS TO TWIN - KLE BRIGHT - LY A -

BOVE. IT'S GOOD - BYE TO MY___ LIT - TLE BOAT OF LOVE.

BOAT OF LOVE. GOOD - BYE,___ LIT - TLE

BOAT.___ GOOD - BYE,___ LIT - TLE BOAT.___

THE NIGHT HAS A THOUSAND EYES

THEME FROM THE PARAMOUNT PICTURE THE NIGHT HAS A THOUSAND EYES

WORDS BY BUDDY BERNIER
MUSIC BY JERRY BRAININ

WON - DROUS___ NIGHT___ THAT HAS A THOU-SAND EYES.___ I'VE

LIVED MY___ LIFE___ WALK-ING THROUGH- A DREAM.___ FOR I

KNEW THAT I WOULD FIND THIS MO-MENT SU - PREME.___ A

NIGHT OF BLISS___ AND TEN - DER SIGHS___

AND THE SMIL - ING DOWN___ OF A THOU-SAND EYES.__

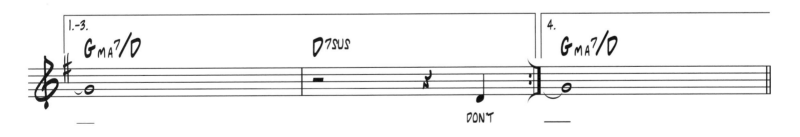

DON'T

JAZZ IMPROV. TO END

SO NICE
(SUMMER SAMBA)

ORIGINAL WORDS AND MUSIC BY MARCOS VALLE
AND PAULO SERGIO VALLE
ENGLISH WORDS BY NORMAN GIMBEL

CD 14

STOMPIN' AT THE SAVOY

WORDS BY ANDY RAZAF
MUSIC BY BENNY GOODMAN, EDGAR SAMPSON
AND CHICK WEBB

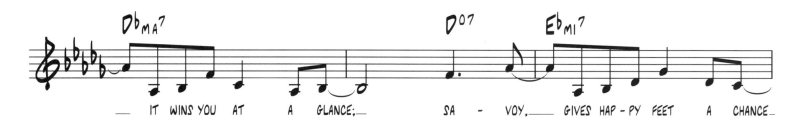

How my heart is sing - in'____

While the band is swing - in'!____

Nev - er tired of roam - in'____ and stomp - in' with you____

At the Sa - voy.____ What joy!____ A per - fect hol - i - day!____

____ Sa - voy,____ where we can glide and sway;

____ Sa - voy,____ there let me stomp a - way____

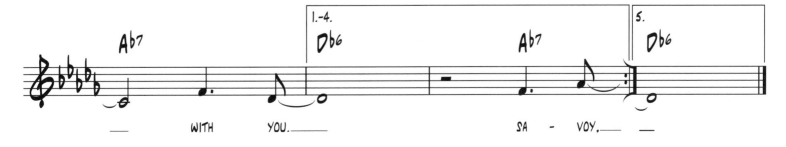

____ with you.____ Sa - voy,____

THERE WILL NEVER BE ANOTHER YOU

FROM THE MOTION PICTURE ICELAND

LYRIC BY MACK GORDON
MUSIC BY HARRY WARREN

YOU ARE TOO BEAUTIFUL

FROM HALLELUJAH, I'M A BUM

WORDS BY LORENZ HART
MUSIC BY RICHARD RODGERS

CD 16

Presenting the Hal Leonard JAZZ PLAY-ALONG SERIES

For use with all B-flat, E-flat, Bass Clef and C instruments, the Jazz Play-Along® Series is the ultimate learning tool for all jazz musicians. With musician-friendly lead sheets, melody cues, and other split-track choices on the included CD, these first-of-a-kind packages help you master improvisation while playing some of the greatest tunes of all time. FOR STUDY, each tune includes a split track with: melody cue with proper style and inflection • professional rhythm tracks • choruses for soloing • removable bass part • removable piano part. FOR PERFORMANCE, each tune also has: an additional full stereo accompaniment track (no melody) • additional choruses for soloing.

1. DUKE ELLINGTON
00841644.........................$16.95

1A. MAIDEN VOYAGE/ALL BLUES
00843158 ....$15.99

2. MILES DAVIS
00841645.........................$16.95

3. THE BLUES
00841646.........................$16.99

4. JAZZ BALLADS
00841691.........................$16.99

5. BEST OF BEBOP
00841689.........................$16.95

6. JAZZ CLASSICS WITH EASY CHANGES
00841690.........................$16.99

7. ESSENTIAL JAZZ STANDARDS
00843000.........................$16.99

8. ANTONIO CARLOS JOBIM AND THE ART OF THE BOSSA NOVA
00843001.........................$16.95

9. DIZZY GILLESPIE
00843002.........................$16.99

10. DISNEY CLASSICS
00843003.........................$16.99

11. RODGERS AND HART FAVORITES
00843004.........................$16.99

12. ESSENTIAL JAZZ CLASSICS
00843005.........................$16.99

13. JOHN COLTRANE
00843006.........................$16.95

14. IRVING BERLIN
00843007.........................$15.99

15. RODGERS & HAMMERSTEIN
00843008.........................$15.99

16. COLE PORTER
00843009.........................$15.95

17. COUNT BASIE
00843010.........................$16.95

18. HAROLD ARLEN
00843011.........................$15.95

19. COOL JAZZ
00843012.........................$15.95

20. CHRISTMAS CAROLS
00843080.........................$14.95

21. RODGERS AND HART CLASSICS
00843014.........................$14.95

22. WAYNE SHORTER
00843015.........................$16.95

23. LATIN JAZZ
00843016.........................$16.95

24. EARLY JAZZ STANDARDS
00843017.........................$14.95

25. CHRISTMAS JAZZ
00843018.........................$16.95

26. CHARLIE PARKER
00843019.........................$16.95

27. GREAT JAZZ STANDARDS
00843020.........................$16.99

28. BIG BAND ERA
00843021.........................$15.99

29. LENNON AND MCCARTNEY
00843022.........................$16.95

30. BLUES' BEST
00843023.........................$15.99

31. JAZZ IN THREE
00843024.........................$15.99

32. BEST OF SWING
00843025.........................$15.99

33. SONNY ROLLINS
00843029.........................$15.95

34. ALL TIME STANDARDS
00843030.........................$15.99

35. BLUESY JAZZ
00843031.........................$16.99

36. HORACE SILVER
00843032.........................$16.99

37. BILL EVANS
00843033.........................$16.95

38. YULETIDE JAZZ
00843034.........................$16.95

39. "ALL THE THINGS YOU ARE" & MORE JEROME KERN SONGS
00843035.........................$15.99

40. BOSSA NOVA
00843036.........................$15.99

41. CLASSIC DUKE ELLINGTON
00843037.........................$16.99

42. GERRY MULLIGAN FAVORITES
00843038.........................$16.99

43. GERRY MULLIGAN CLASSICS
00843039.........................$16.95

44. OLIVER NELSON
00843040.........................$16.95

45. JAZZ AT THE MOVIES
00843041.........................$15.99

46. BROADWAY JAZZ STANDARDS
00843042.........................$15.99

47. CLASSIC JAZZ BALLADS
00843043.........................$15.99

48. BEBOP CLASSICS
00843044.........................$16.99

49. MILES DAVIS STANDARDS
00843045.........................$16.95

50. GREAT JAZZ CLASSICS
00843046.........................$15.99

51. UP-TEMPO JAZZ
00843047.........................$15.99

52. STEVIE WONDER
00843048.........................$16.99

53. RHYTHM CHANGES
00843049.........................$15.99

54. "MOONLIGHT IN VERMONT" AND OTHER GREAT STANDARDS
00843050.........................$15.99

55. BENNY GOLSON
00843052.........................$15.95

56. "GEORGIA ON MY MIND" & OTHER SONGS BY HOAGY CARMICHAEL
00843056 ....$15.99

57. VINCE GUARALDI
00843057.........................$16.99

58. MORE LENNON AND MCCARTNEY
00843059.........................$15.99

59. SOUL JAZZ
00843060.........................$15.99

60. DEXTER GORDON
00843061 ....$15.95

61. MONGO SANTAMARIA
00843062.........................$15.95

62. JAZZ-ROCK FUSION
00843063.........................$16.99

63. CLASSICAL JAZZ
00843064 ....$14.95

64. TV TUNES
00843065 ....$14.95

65. SMOOTH JAZZ
00843066 ....$16.99

66. A CHARLIE BROWN CHRISTMAS
00843067 ....$16.99

67. CHICK COREA
00843068 ....$15.95

68. CHARLES MINGUS
00843069 ....$16.95

69. CLASSIC JAZZ
00843071 ....$15.99

70. THE DOORS
00843072 ....$14.95

71. COLE PORTER CLASSICS
00843073 ....$14.95

72. CLASSIC JAZZ BALLADS
00843074 ....$15.99

73. JAZZ/BLUES
00843075 ....$14.95

74. BEST JAZZ CLASSICS
00843076 ....$15.99

75. PAUL DESMOND
00843077 ....$14.95

76. BROADWAY JAZZ BALLADS
00843078 ....$15.99

77. JAZZ ON BROADWAY
00843079 ....$15.99

78. STEELY DAN
00843070 ....$14.99

79. MILES DAVIS CLASSICS
00843081 ....$15.99

80. JIMI HENDRIX
00843083 ....$15.99

81. FRANK SINATRA – CLASSICS
00843084 ....$15.99

82. FRANK SINATRA – STANDARDS
00843085 ....$15.99

83. ANDREW LLOYD WEBBER
00843104 ....$14.95

84. BOSSA NOVA CLASSICS
00843105 ....$14.95

85. MOTOWN HITS
00843109 ....$14.95

86. BENNY GOODMAN
00843110 ....$14.95

87. DIXIELAND
00843111 ....$14.95

88. DUKE ELLINGTON FAVORITES
00843112 ....$14.95

89. IRVING BERLIN FAVORITES
00843113 ....$14.95

90. THELONIOUS MONK CLASSICS
00841262 ....$16.99

91. THELONIOUS MONK FAVORITES
00841263 ....$16.99

92. LEONARD BERNSTEIN
00450134 ....$15.99

93. DISNEY FAVORITES
00843142 ....$14.99

94. RAY
00843143 ....$14.99

95. JAZZ AT THE LOUNGE
00843144 ....V$14.99

96. LATIN JAZZ STANDARDS
00843145 ....$14.99

97. MAYBE I'M AMAZED✱
00843148 ....$15.99

98. DAVE FRISHBERG
00843149 ....$15.99

99. SWINGING STANDARDS
00843150 ....$14.99

100. LOUIS ARMSTRONG
00740423 ....$15.99

101. BUD POWELL
00843152 ....$14.99

102. JAZZ POP
00843153 ....$14.99

**103. ON GREEN DOLPHIN STREET
& OTHER JAZZ CLASSICS**
00843154 ....$14.99

104. ELTON JOHN
00843155 ....$14.99

105. SOULFUL JAZZ
00843151 ....$15.99

106. SLO' JAZZ
00843117 ....$14.99

107. MOTOWN CLASSICS
00843116 ....$14.99

108. JAZZ WALTZ
00843159 ....$15.99

109. OSCAR PETERSON
00843160 ....$16.99

110. JUST STANDARDS
00843161 ....$15.99

111. COOL CHRISTMAS
00843162 ....$15.99

112. PAQUITO D'RIVERA – LATIN JAZZ✱
48020662 ....$16.99

113. PAQUITO D'RIVERA – BRAZILIAN JAZZ✱
48020663 ....$19.99

114. MODERN JAZZ QUARTET FAVORITES
00843163 ....$15.99

115. THE SOUND OF MUSIC
00843164 ....$15.99

116. JACO PASTORIUS
00843165 ....$15.99

117. ANTONIO CARLOS JOBIM – MORE HITS
00843166 ....$15.99

118. BIG JAZZ STANDARDS COLLECTION
00843167 ....$27.50

119. JELLY ROLL MORTON
00843168 ....$15.99

120. J.S. BACH
00843169 ....$15.99

121. DJANGO REINHARDT
00843170 ....$15.99

122. PAUL SIMON
00843182 ....$16.99

123. BACHARACH & DAVID
00843185 ....$15.99

124. JAZZ-ROCK HORN HITS
00843186 ....$15.99

126. COUNT BASIE CLASSICS
00843157 ....$15.99

127. CHUCK MANGIONE
00843188 ....$15.99

132. STAN GETZ ESSENTIALS
00843193 ....$15.99

133. STAN GETZ FAVORITES
00843194 ....$15.99

134. NURSERY RHYMES✱
00843196 ....$17.99

135. JEFF BECK
00843197 ....$15.99

136. NAT ADDERLEY
00843198 ....$15.99

137. WES MONTGOMERY
00843199 ....$15.99

138. FREDDIE HUBBARD
00843200 ....$15.99

139. JULIAN "CANNONBALL" ADDERLEY
00843201 ....$15.99

141. BILL EVANS STANDARDS
00843156 ....$15.99

150. JAZZ IMPROV BASICS
00843195 ....$19.99

151. MODERN JAZZ QUARTET CLASSICS
00843209 ....$15.99

157. HYMNS
00843217 ....$15.99

162. BIG CHRISTMAS COLLECTION
00843221 ....$24.99

Prices, contents, and availability subject to change without notice.

FOR MORE INFORMATION,
SEE YOUR LOCAL MUSIC DEALER,
OR WRITE TO:

HAL•LEONARD®
CORPORATION
7777 W. BLUEMOUND RD. P.O. BOX 13819
MILWAUKEE, WISCONSIN 53213
For complete songlists and more,
visit Hal Leonard online at
www.halleonard.com

0811

✱These CDs do not include split tracks.

Pro Vocal® Series

SONGBOOK & SOUND-ALIKE CD
SING 8 GREAT SONGS
WITH A PROFESSIONAL BAND

Whether you're a karaoke singer or an auditioning professional, the Pro Vocal® series is for you! Unlike most karaoke packs, each book in the Pro Vocal Series contains the lyrics, melody, and chord symbols for eight hit songs. The CD contains demos for listening, and separate backing tracks so you can sing along. The CD is playable on any CD player, but it is also enhanced so PC and Mac computer users can adjust the recording to any pitch without changing the tempo! Perfect for home rehearsal, parties, auditions, corporate events, and gigs without a backup band.

WOMEN'S EDITIONS

00740247	**1. Broadway Songs**	$14.95
00740249	**2. Jazz Standards**	$14.95
00740246	**3. Contemporary Hits**	$14.95
00740277	**4. '80s Gold**	$12.95
00740299	**5. Christmas Standards**	$15.95
00740281	**6. Disco Fever**	$12.95
00740279	**7. R&B Super Hits**	$12.95
00740309	**8. Wedding Gems**	$12.95
00740409	**9. Broadway Standards**	$14.95
00740348	**10. Andrew Lloyd Webber**	$14.95
00740344	**11. Disney's Best**	$14.99
00740378	**12. Ella Fitzgerald**	$14.95
00740350	**14. Musicals of Boublil & Schönberg**	$14.95
00740377	**15. Kelly Clarkson**	$14.95
00740342	**16. Disney Favorites**	$14.99
00740353	**17. Jazz Ballads**	$14.99
00740376	**18. Jazz Vocal Standards**	$16.99
00740375	**20. Hannah Montana**	$16.95
00740354	**21. Jazz Favorites**	$14.99
00740374	**22. Patsy Cline**	$14.95
00740369	**23. Grease**	$14.95
00740367	**25. ABBA**	$14.95
00740365	**26. Movie Songs**	$14.95
00740360	**28. High School Musical 1 & 2**	$14.95
00740363	**29. Torch Songs**	$14.95
00740379	**30. Hairspray**	$14.95
00740380	**31. Top Hits**	$14.95
00740384	**32. Hits of the '70s**	$14.95
00740388	**33. Billie Holiday**	$14.95
00740389	**34. The Sound of Music**	$15.99
00740390	**35. Contemporary Christian**	$14.95
00740392	**36. Wicked**	$15.99
00740393	**37. More Hannah Montana**	$14.95
00740394	**38. Miley Cyrus**	$14.95
00740396	**39. Christmas Hits**	$15.95
00740410	**40. Broadway Classics**	$14.95
00740415	**41. Broadway Favorites**	$14.99
00740416	**42. Great Standards You Can Sing**	$14.99
00740417	**43. Singable Standards**	$14.99
00740418	**44. Favorite Standards**	$14.99
00740419	**45. Sing Broadway**	$14.99
00740420	**46. More Standards**	$14.99
00740421	**47. Timeless Hits**	$14.99
00740422	**48. Easygoing R&B**	$14.99
00740424	**49. Taylor Swift**	$15.99
00740425	**50. From This Moment On**	$14.99
00740426	**51. Great Standards Collection**	$19.99
00740430	**52. Worship Favorites**	$14.99
00740434	**53. Lullabyes**	$14.99
00740438	**54. Lady Gaga**	$14.99
00740444	**55. Amy Winehouse**	$14.99
00740445	**56. Adele**	$14.99

MEN'S EDITIONS

00740248	**1. Broadway Songs**	$14.95
00740250	**2. Jazz Standards**	$14.95
00740251	**3. Contemporary Hits**	$14.99
00740278	**4. '80s Gold**	$12.95
00740298	**5. Christmas Standards**	$15.95
00740280	**6. R&B Super Hits**	$12.95
00740282	**7. Disco Fever**	$12.95
00740310	**8. Wedding Gems**	$12.95
00740411	**9. Broadway Greats**	$14.99
00740333	**10. Elvis Presley – Volume 1**	$14.95
00740349	**11. Andrew Lloyd Webber**	$14.95
00740345	**12. Disney's Best**	$14.95
00740347	**13. Frank Sinatra Classics**	$14.95
00740334	**14. Lennon & McCartney**	$14.99
00740335	**16. Elvis Presley – Volume 2**	$14.99
00740343	**17. Disney Favorites**	$14.99
00740351	**18. Musicals of Boublil & Schönberg**	$14.95
00740346	**20. Frank Sinatra Standards**	$14.95
00740358	**22. Great Standards**	$14.99
00740336	**23. Elvis Presley**	$14.99
00740341	**24. Duke Ellington**	$14.99
00740359	**26. Pop Standards**	$14.99
00740362	**27. Michael Bublé**	$14.95
00740364	**29. Torch Songs**	$14.95
00740366	**30. Movie Songs**	$14.95
00740368	**31. Hip Hop Hits**	$14.95
00740370	**32. Grease**	$14.95
00740371	**33. Josh Groban**	$14.95
00740373	**34. Billy Joel**	$14.99
00740381	**35. Hits of the '50s**	$14.95
00740382	**36. Hits of the '60s**	$14.95
00740383	**37. Hits of the '70s**	$14.95
00740385	**38. Motown**	$14.95
00740386	**39. Hank Williams**	$14.95
00740387	**40. Neil Diamond**	$14.95
00740391	**41. Contemporary Christian**	$14.95
00740397	**42. Christmas Hits**	$15.95
00740399	**43. Ray**	$14.95
00740400	**44. The Rat Pack Hits**	$14.99
00740401	**45. Songs in the Style of Nat "King" Cole**	$14.99
00740402	**46. At the Lounge**	$14.95
00740403	**47. The Big Band Singer**	$14.95
00740404	**48. Jazz Cabaret Songs**	$14.99
00740405	**49. Cabaret Songs**	$14.99
00740406	**50. Big Band Standards**	$14.99
00740412	**51. Broadway's Best**	$14.99
00740427	**52. Great Standards Collection**	$19.99
00740431	**53. Worship Favorites**	$14.99
00740435	**54. Barry Manilow**	$14.99
00740436	**55. Lionel Richie**	$14.99
00740439	**56. Michael Bublé – Crazy Love**	$14.99
00740441	**57. Johnny Cash**	$14.99
00740442	**58. Bruno Mars**	$14.99

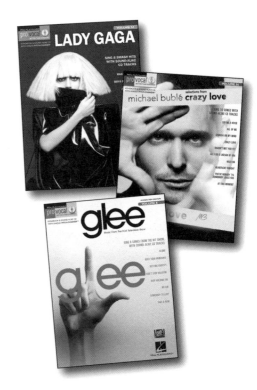

MIXED EDITIONS

These editions feature songs for both male and female voices.

00740311	**1. Wedding Duets**	$12.95
00740398	**2. Enchanted**	$14.95
00740407	**3. Rent**	$14.95
00740408	**4. Broadway Favorites**	$14.99
00740413	**5. South Pacific**	$15.99
00740414	**6. High School Musical 3**	$14.99
00740429	**7. Christmas Carols**	$14.99
00740437	**8. Glee**	$15.99
00740440	**9. More Songs from Glee**	$19.99
00740443	**10. Even More Songs from Glee**	$15.99

FOR MORE INFORMATION, SEE YOUR LOCAL MUSIC DEALER, OR WRITE TO:

HAL•LEONARD®
CORPORATION

7777 W. BLUEMOUND RD. P.O. BOX 13819 MILWAUKEE, WI 53213

Prices, contents, & availability subject to change without notice.

Visit Hal Leonard online at
www.halleonard.com

0811